These questions are answered by:

All your answers are not wrong
All your answers are not always right
All come from your bright or dark thoughts
All come truly, deeply from your heart and soul
And all come to define who you are at this very moment

DAY 1

What is your opinion about it?

DAY 2

There's a fish swimming at sea... [continue the sentence]

DAY 3

What's your reaction to all of this?

DAY 4

How do you deal with those stories about you?

DAY 5

How do you deal with the other people who think you're a bad man/woman?

DAY 6

If you could just go back to the start, would you? Why? Why not?

DAY 7

What would you do if you woke up one morning with a tail?

DAY 8

If you were lost in the woods and it got dark, what would you do?

DAY 9

Say something about your own experiences with your family.

DAY 10

What is the worst thing you've ever had to go through?

DAY 11

What makes you feel so bad about it?

DAY 12

What would you do if a friend borrows things from you but never returns them?

DAY 13

How do you know when to go into the sunset?

DAY 14

It was the last day of her life… [continue the sentence]

DAY 15

Say something that makes you think you're nice.

DAY 16

Are you afraid of snakes? Why? Why not?

DAY 17

What is your favorite color?

DAY 18

List of things that needs adjusting

DAY 19

What do you think about when you're by yourself?

DAY 20

What is the first thing you do before taking a shower?

DAY 21

Would you rather have a dog or a llama? Why?

DAY 22

What would be your favorite holiday?

DAY 23

Say something about the way you do things.

DAY 24

List of things that are tricky

What would you think if you were given the power to change an entire continent of this size?

Will you say you were right? Why or why not?

Would you rather be a woman or a man?

DAY 28

What have you done that shows you that you are good?

DAY 29

What's the one thing that you wish to keep out of the public eye?

DAY 30

What type of car would you like to own?

DAY 31

What medium would your life best be shown as? A movie? A television series? A cartoon? What genre would a movie about your life fall under? Comedy? Romance?

DAY 32

Who would you choose to portray you in a movie about your life?

DAY 33

How would you handle things with someone you care about, not just in the moment, but over time?

DAY 34

Write a letter to the person you love most.

DAY 35

Would you ever start a fight with a coworker?

DAY 36

If you had to choose only one thing to be worried about when traveling, what would it be?

DAY 37

Who's your greatest asset?

DAY 38

Do you have any tattoos? What do they mean? If you haven't, would you ever get some?

DAY 39

Why do you think it's going to be so hard?

DAY 40

What do you remember about your mother?

DAY 41

If you had to choose one thing as an important reason for your decision, do you think love was the most important factor?

DAY 42

If you had to choose one thing in life to have your parents worry about, what would it be?

DAY 43

Where do you think you will be in a year?

DAY 44

What are some nutritious foods that you like?

DAY 45

What is a mistake you've made?

What's your plan for a future of self-discovery?

What is the best thing about a movie that you have never seen?

If you could teach yourself, what would it be?

DAY 49

How do you deal with people who want to try to cheat on you?

DAY 50

What makes you smile the most?

DAY 51

What is the one thing we must avoid doing if we want to have a long-lasting and healthy relationship?

DAY 52

What is one thing that makes you more likely to take action in an area where there is uncertainty?

DAY 53

What time period you would like to be born in?

DAY 54

How do you find the best time to write?

DAY 55

What happens on the other side of the door?

DAY 56

Why does it exist?

DAY 57

How would you describe the feeling of being alive at the moment?

What would it take to make you change your mind?

What can you do to save a life?

Would you rather have a glass of water or a soda?

DAY 61

What is the one thing people miss?

DAY 62

What is the most significant event that happened during your professional career?

DAY 63

If you had to choose one thing you hate about yourself in life, what would it be?

DAY 64

How do you plan to put the lessons you've learned into action going forward?

____

____

____

____

____

DAY 65

If you could have your cake and eat it too, would you do it? Why?

____

____

____

____

DAY 66

Say something about your interests.

DAY 67

List of things that have made family and relationships more difficult over time

---

DAY 68

If you could spend the next 20 years, how would you spend it?

DAY 69

Is the popularity of such weird and utterly bizarre ideas overrated? Why?

DAY 70

If you had to live a life in any other universe, would you live it? Why?

DAY 71

If you could have anything in the world, what would it be?

DAY 72

List of things that can be done with

DAY 73

What is more important to you to honor those to whom you owe the most?

DAY 74

List of things that you are looking for

DAY 75

How do you deal with the way it feels in front of you?

DAY 76

If you had to have a conversation with a stranger for a week, what words would you use?

DAY 77

How did you meet your first boyfriend or girlfriend?

DAY 78

What does your child like to do when he/she is angry?

DAY 79

Do you sometimes feel sad you didn't do something to help? Why?

DAY 80

What made you the person you are right now?

DAY 81

What would your ideal life look like?

DAY 82

What is your most terrifying question?

DAY 83

What is your favorite color combination?

DAY 84

*Why do you think so many people who are struggling or feel
they are failing at something?*

DAY 85

What is your least ideal outcome?

DAY 86

What's your favorite activity to do?

DAY 87

What's the dumbest thing you've done on the road?

DAY 88

How do you deal with a system that's more geared toward creating a kind of self-regulation for people so that there's no need for them to do things?

DAY 89

What are some things that you have done that made you happy at that time?

DAY 90

What character trait do you most dislike in yourself?

DAY 91

Are you more of a cat person or a dog person? Why?

DAY 92

*Would you rather have a good haircut but take a lot of time
and effort or do you prefer the quick option with so-so result?*

DAY 93

List of things that you always find yourself needing to do

DAY 94

Who would you want to play you in a movie of your life and why? Who could play the other important roles? What songs would you choose for the soundtrack? Create the play list.

DAY 95

If you could be in two places at once, which two places would you choose?

DAY 96

Why do you think it's funny?

DAY 97

If you could take a second to pause and ask yourself, what will be the question?

DAY 98

What's on your bucket list this year?

DAY 99

If you had to choose two of your favorite authors to write about, who would you choose and why?

DAY 100

*If you had to choose only three people to be on your team, who
would they be?*

DAY 101

What animal do you identify with most closely? Why?

DAY 102

*If you could only use one word to describe yourself, what
would it be?*

DAY 103

How would you know when your change is complete and you are no longer the same person as you were?

DAY 104

Do you ever miss home? Why? Why not?

DAY 105

What is one thing you have in common with the 'good guy'?

DAY 106

How do you dance?

DAY 107

How did your day go and why do you work?

DAY 108

Would you rather eat food that grows in the sun or food that grows in the water?

DAY 109

What are the three most valuable things you've heard in your life?

DAY 110

What exactly are you getting for that money?

DAY 111

If you had to choose one thing that would make or break your life for the next month, what would it be?

DAY 112

Would you rather you didn't do it?

DAY 113

What do you think makes a good leader?

DAY 114

What's the one thing that you wish you were able to be honest with?

DAY 115

What song really makes you happy?

DAY 116

If you had to choose one thing as your greatest triumph and one thing that you felt was your greatest failure, what would it be?

DAY 117

List of things that you can do to honor someone you lost

DAY 118

List of things that looked too much alike

DAY 119

Is that something you would use yourself? Why?

DAY 120

*Talk about the year that was. Are you happy with it, or do you
wish you could've done some things differently?*

DAY 121

At what point did you realize you were doing the right thing?

DAY 122

How would you describe the feeling of being in a room with someone when they are angry at you for something that you did?

DAY 123

List of things that you would change as a result of that

DAY 124

What did you do today to impress the person you love?

DAY 125

What do you prefer to read in bed?

DAY 126

*Are you looking for a certain feeling in your life or do you look for a
particular solution in any situation? Why? Why not?*

DAY 127

When was the last time you walked into a room and felt like you fit into it?

DAY 128

Name three habits that you do on the job that people don't know you're doing?

DAY 129

What makes you feel energized?

DAY 130

If you could only have one piece of clothing for your life, what would it be and why?

DAY 131

If you were in the band, what instrument would you be playing?

DAY 132

List of things that I am looking for in life

DAY 133

What book setting would you like to visit, if you could?

DAY 134

How do you stop complaining and getting over it?

DAY 135

If you could do anything in the world, what would you want to do?

DAY 136

If you could pick the two things you wanted to change about your childhood, what would they be?

DAY 137

What do you do in your downtime?

DAY 138

What if you can no longer use your hands? How do you think would you be able to live?

DAY 139

How do you eat dinner?

DAY 140

What do people do when you're not around?

DAY 141

*If you had to pick a person to be the person who is the best of
the best, who would it be?*

DAY 142

What do you think your life will be like ten years from now?

DAY 143

Would you rather have a society in which the only language that matters is the one that you use? Why?

DAY 144

What is the one thing you can tell that no one will ever believe?

DAY 145

How can you overcome your fears?

DAY 146

What can you do to make you feel better about what happened?

DAY 147

List of things that affect your mood

DAY 148

How do you make an effective decision?

DAY 149

What do you like best about the human race?

DAY 150

What happens when you get mad at someone who doesn't like your gift?

DAY 151

What's the strangest thing people have ever said to you?

DAY 152

Would you rather the world be at peace or at war?

DAY 153

If you had to choose one friend to include in your life, who would it be and why?

List of things that makes one smile

What is one thing that you miss?

Why do you not want men to help you?

DAY 157

What would you prefer to drink?

DAY 158

Why does it bother you so much?

DAY 159

What are your ideas that come to mind?

What's the best thing about being able to look at yourself in the mirror?

What have you learned or experienced from the conversation?

List of things that you don't need

DAY 163

What is one of your most personal hopes and dreams?

DAY 164

What is one of the most valuable skills that you could improve?

DAY 165

Do you think your life is hard? Why?

DAY 166

Why is it not wise to squander your money?

DAY 167

Would you rather have a friend, who is not a robot by any means, ask a few silly questions about the weather or give a random quiz, or just ask and answer your own questions?

DAY 168

How would you describe the feeling of being royalty?

DAY 169

List of things that one can say about it

____

____

____

____

____

DAY 170

If you could go back in time, would you go back and do a different thing?

____

____

____

____

DAY 171

Would you rather know?

DAY 172

Why is your life like that?

DAY 173

If you had to choose one thing that is important about your life, what would it be?

DAY 174

What did you get from this experience?

DAY 175

If you could meet your future self, who would it be?

DAY 176

What is one thing that you have learned in the past two months that could be improved or be made more effective?

DAY 177

What do you think it was?

DAY 178

What is the most unprofessional thing you've seen someone do?

DAY 179

Are you someone who agrees to disagree? Why?

DAY 180

There's an Llama in the garden... [continue the sentence]

DAY 181

How do you deal with the next person who you want to do you harm?

DAY 182

Would you rather have the world get worse or continue living in the same way?

DAY 183

How would you describe the feeling of being safe when everyone hates you?

DAY 184

What might happen if you've tried?

DAY 185

What is the one thing you have learned about yourself that has helped you through?

DAY 186

Why do you feel you are misunderstood, misunderstood, and misunderstood and why?

DAY 187

How do you feel when you want something very badly and you cannot have it? Why is this so important to have?

DAY 188

What do you think is wrong with society today?

DAY 189

How would you describe the feeling of being lonely?

DAY 190

What does your daughter look for in a boyfriend/girlfriend?

DAY 191

Say something that really hurts your feelings.

DAY 192

What are you looking for when it comes to romance?

DAY 193

What things would be different if you did things differently?

DAY 194

What's the best birthday present you ever received?

DAY 195

What's your most weird question?

DAY 196

List of things that you want to point out

DAY 197

What would you do if an hour before the party you remember you don't have a gift?

DAY 198

Say something that you've always been able to find a way to make people happy

DAY 199

What's so terrible about the world that you don't believe it is worth trying to fix?

DAY 200

List of perfumes to freshen up after

DAY 201

List of things that I do on the weekends

DAY 202

Do you choose to be dependent on others? Why? Why not?

DAY 203

Would you rather take a vow of celibacy or take a vow of silence? Why?

DAY 204

List of things that stopped working

What would you do if that's the way you felt?

What's the best concert you've ever been to?

What were the two reasons for your success?

Say something about yourself, but don't say too much.

What is the one thing you don't do well?

You're outside for a whole day, what would you do?

DAY 211

When did you last see someone you loved?

DAY 212

When was the last time you got a cold?

DAY 213

How would you describe the feeling of being wrong?

DAY 214

Who is one person you would never want to have dinner with?

DAY 215

A white rose left out at sea… [continue the sentence]

DAY 216

Would you rather be at home or would you rather be at the office?

DAY 217

If you could take a step and give the love you need in your life,
would you and why?

DAY 218

What animals are you most afraid of?

DAY 219

Why do you think people feel so comfortable getting back into
the business and getting back to making money?

DAY 220

What were the differences between you, when you were a little kid, and now, when you're old enough to do it?

DAY 221

Say something about your favorite character.

DAY 222

Where do you see yourself in years?

DAY 223

Do you ever feel like you're being controlled? Why?

DAY 224

Would you rather they not and if they do, would you like them to go away?

DAY 225

What can you say to a stranger in an elevator to make that stranger feel at ease?

DAY 226

Do you prefer to be the center of attention or be left alone?

DAY 227

What's your first memory of the internet?

DAY 228

What is the best thing to wear under your t-shirt?

DAY 229

What would it take to get it to become a reality?

DAY 230

What are your favorite activities? Why?

DAY 231

How many times per day do you think you might run out of money?

DAY 232

Do you have a sense of responsibility? How?

DAY 233

What do you think about others?

DAY 234

If you could give yourself one piece of advice for anyone, what would it be?

DAY 235

What is a thing that you do at home in your spare time?

DAY 236

Who would you trust to do things the way you believe they should?

DAY 237

What do you consider your greatest achievement?

DAY 238

Would you rather have your cake or have the world burn?

DAY 239

What is the earliest photograph of yourself that you have that you remember when it was taken?

DAY 240

What is one thing you would like to do before you die?

DAY 241

Would you rather I do that or talk to you?

DAY 242

Would you describe your work process?

DAY 243

What is the one thing that concerns you?

If you had to choose one thing in this life to do over and over again, would you do it?

How would you describe the feeling of being never being satisfied in a relationship?

How do you feel about Thanksgiving? What are you thankful for?

DAY 247

What's your favorite trip so far?

DAY 248

Would you rather go into hibernation? Why?

DAY 249

*If you could choose a time and place and do it over again,
what would you tell yourself?*

DAY 250

What drives you to get out of bed every morning?

DAY 251

What are your happy hours like with friends?

DAY 252

Explain to a doctor what would be helpful during an office visit.

DAY 253

List of things that didn't quite pan out

DAY 254

What's one song that reminds you of your first love?

DAY 255

What do you dream of?

DAY 256

Describe how communication has changed in the last 30 years.

DAY 257

Why do you come back here?

DAY 258

What is one thing you have in common with your favorite superhero?

DAY 259

Would you be a different person today if you had a different childhood? How?

DAY 260

What was it like to come out of your shell?

DAY 261

How do you cope with people who are trying to convince you that the statement you were saying was true?

DAY 262

If you could start your journey today, would you do it? Why?

DAY 263

Would you ever be in a committed romantic relationship? How is it?

DAY 264

How will you know what you are good at?

DAY 265

Would you rather do or not do?

DAY 266

List of things that you should never do

DAY 267

If you could run out to any restaurant right now with more than enough money, where would you go?

DAY 268

What's on the agenda for the day?

DAY 269

Would you rather live in a world where you are not constantly having to remind yourself to think?

DAY 270

What is most important to you in all situations?

DAY 271

Would you rather be positive or negative?

DAY 272

List of things that can stop your working memory

DAY 273

What are the two sides of your story?

DAY 274

How would you describe the feeling of needing to have?

DAY 275

What causes you to feel bad about yourself?

DAY 276

*Why your favorite things are those which cause you to have an
idea?*

DAY 277

Do you think you're already happy with who you are right now,
or do you think you could be so much more?

DAY 278

Would you rather have him/her or be him/her? Why?

DAY 279

What is one thing you as a sports fan cannot live without?

DAY 280

If you could be any celebrity, who would you be and why?

DAY 281

Describe techniques or methods that could help teachers do their job more effectively.

DAY 282

Are you competitive? Tell me about a competition that you participated in.

DAY 283

What's your favorite color that has lots of shades?

DAY 284

What's a simple way to brighten someone's day?

DAY 285

What would you do if you won a million dollars?

DAY 286

List of things that I want to buy

DAY 287

Why do you keep doing the same thing over and over again
and expecting different results?

DAY 288

Have you ever felt like a fraud?

DAY 289

What's one thing you want your child to get right at an early age?

DAY 290

List of things that would make you slow

DAY 291

Would you rather have you do it? Why?

When did you get your first tattoo? Why?

Which would you choose between someone who would put the interests of people first or someone who would put themselves first?

Is it better to live alone or in a family?

DAY 295

How can you have a good week?

DAY 296

How would you live your day if you do not have the freedom of expression?

DAY 297

Would you rather never touch an electronic device again or never touch a human again? Why?

DAY 298

List of things that you want to make in the future

DAY 299

If you could have one conversation with anyone in the world, who would it be with?

DAY 300

What types of relationships do you want to have?

DAY 301

What are you least ashamed of?

DAY 302

If you could only eat three foods for the rest of your life what would it be?

DAY 303

What do you call a guy who is trying to get rich quick?

DAY 304

List of things that you would like to achieve in life

DAY 305

How would you describe the feeling of being in charge?

DAY 306

How would you describe the feeling of being like one with the heavens?

DAY 307

What happened when that conversation happened?

____

____

____

____

DAY 308

How do you define your own self-worth?

____

____

____

____

DAY 309

List of things that can be desired

DAY 310

What is the hardest decision that you had to make?

DAY 311

What are your biggest challenges?

DAY 312

What happens when something like that happens?

DAY 313

What is most important to you to make your work more satisfying?

DAY 314

What do you think about people polluting the environment?

DAY 315

How do you deal with a loss like that?

DAY 316

What do you remember about your childhood?

DAY 317

What do you expect?

DAY 318

Do you wish you died when you were young or do you wish you were born?

DAY 319

Describe the most effective teacher you've ever had.

DAY 320

What is the one thing you have learned throughout your career that will be the biggest difference in your life now?

DAY 321

If you could be more than the sum of your experiences, what would it be?

DAY 322

List of things that you liked

DAY 323

How do you deal with people who are not willing to take the time to learn how to do what you want?

DAY 324

If you could take one lesson from your career, what would it be?

DAY 325

Would you rather fight a lion, a wolf or a bear? Why?

DAY 326

Remember when you felt like you were an outsider? What do you feel?

DAY 327

Has anyone ever actually tried to correct your spelling? What is your reaction?

DAY 328

Have you ever been cheated on?

DAY 329

What's your masterpiece?

DAY 330

What would happen if it really did rain cats and dogs?

DAY 331

Why are you attracted to him/her?

DAY 332

How did your child feel when they made a mistake?

DAY 333

What is something you think about every day?

DAY 334

Is there someone at work that makes you feel uncomfortable?

DAY 335

How would you like your legacy to be remembered?

DAY 336

What is one thing you wish you knew before starting this journey?

DAY 337

What is the one thing you find yourself doing everyday that you don't enjoy doing?

DAY 338

What are the 3 things that will make you feel alive when you least expect them?

DAY 339

Can you picture yourself in the shoes of any of the protagonists?

DAY 340

How do you deal with the pressure of growing pains?

DAY 341

What was your favorite time of the month?

DAY 342

What would your dream ice cream flavor be?

DAY 343

What is a safe place that you wish to live in right now?

DAY 344

What is the one thing you could change about your country?

DAY 345

What is your own definition of insanity?

DAY 346

Would you rather be the hunter or the hunted? Why?

DAY 347

If you could write a book, would you and why?

DAY 348

What is the one thing you won't change about yourself?

DAY 349

List of things that threaten human existence

DAY 350

Tell me about an embarrassing moment in your life that is now funny looking back on it.

DAY 351

List of things that you have interpreted

DAY 352

What are one truth and one lie about your personality?

DAY 353

Give me an example of a time when a suggestion you made was used.

DAY 354

What are your favorite foods to eat with your hands?

DAY 355

How to get your date's attention?

DAY 356

What did you do this morning at work?

DAY 357

If you could be anybody, who would you be?

DAY 358

Have you ever had someone else pay for things? Why?

DAY 359

What's the next step for you?

DAY 360

If you could be any fish, what would you be and why?

DAY 361

If you designed clothes, what would they look like?

DAY 362

What exactly are you here for?

DAY 363

When did you experience your "worst feeling in the world"?

DAY 364

When was the last time you made an investment that made you feel like you had some control over your future?

DAY 365

What if you were asked to cry right now? What would you cry about?

DAY 366

What makes you lose track of time?

www.ingramcontent.com/pod-product-compliance
Lightning Source LLC
Chambersburg PA
CBHW022105050726
47591CB00002B/672